BASEBALL HALL OF FAMERS BY POSITION

DAVID FURGESS

First Edition 2013
First published in the USA in December 2013 by
Shibe Park Publishing
All Rights Reserved

SPP-002

No part of this book may be reproduced without written permission of the publisher

Shibe Park Publishing
PO Box 522
Milford, CT
06460 USA

INTRODUCTION

My intention for this book was pretty basic. I just wanted to have a simple, easy to access book to have on my coffee table that had all of Major League Baseball's Hall Of Fame players by position with a concise overview of their career statistics. I figured this would service me in arguments with friends and family about who belongs in the Hall Of Fame and who does not. It would also serve in comparing Hall Of Famers at a particular position.

To be honest I looked around in book stores and online for a book of this type. When I couldn't find it, I just figured I would do it myself. I hope this book will be of service in settling those Hall Of Fame related arguments in your household.

David Furgess
Plainfield, CT
11-20-13

CATCHERS

**Johnny Bench
Yogi Berra
Roger Bresnahan
Roy Campanella
Mickey Cochrane
Bill Dickey
Buck Ewing
Rick Ferrell
Carlton Fisk
Gabby Hartnett
Ernie Lombardi
Ray Schalk**

David Furgess

Johnny Bench
Cincinnati Reds (1967-1983)

AVG (.267) AB (7658)
HR (389)
RBI (1376)
Hits (2048)
Runs (1091)
SLG (.476)
OBP (.345)
SB (68)

Yogi Berra
New York Yankees-New York Mets
1946-1965)

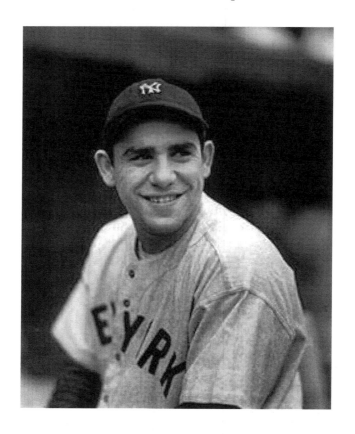

AVG (.285) AB (7555)
HR (358)
RBI (1430)
Hits (2150)
Runs (1175)
SLG (.482)
OBP (.350)
SB (30)

Roger Bresnahan
Washington Senators, Chicago Orphans, Baltimore Orioles, New York Giants, St. Louis Cardinals, Chicago Cubs (1897-1915)

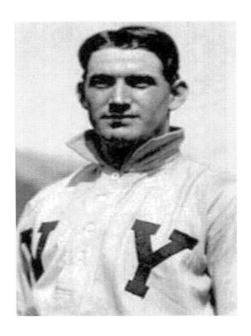

AVG (.279) AB (4481)
HR (26)
RBI (530)
Hits (1252)
Runs (682)
SLG (.377)
OBP (.386)
SB (212)

Roy Campenella
Brooklyn Dodgers
(1948-1957)

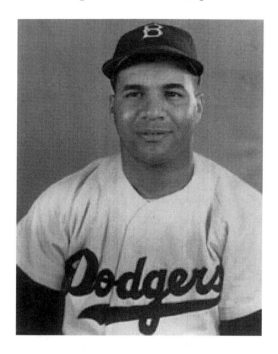

AVG (.276) AB (4205)
HR (242)
RBI (856)
Hits (1161)
Runs (627)
SLG (.500)
OBP (.362)
SB (25)

Gary Carter
Montreal Expos, New York Mets, San Francisco Giants, Los Angeles Dodgers (1974-1992)

AVG (.262) AB (7971)
HR (324)
RBI (1225)
Hits (2092)
Runs (1025)
SLG (.439)
OBP (.335)
SB (39)

Mickey Cochrane
Philadelphia Athletics, Detroit Tigers (1925-1937)

AVG (.320) AB (5169)
HR (119)
RBI (832)
Hits (1652)
Runs (1041)
SLG (.478)
OBP (.419)
SB (64)

Bill Dickey
New York Yankees
(1928-1946)

AVG (.313) AB (6300)
HR (202)
RBI (1209)
Hits (1969)
Runs (930)
SLG (.486)
OBP (.382)
SB (36)

Buck Ewing
Troy Trojans, New York Gothams, New York Giants, Cleveland Spiders, Cincinnati Reds (1880-1987)

AVG (.303) AB (5363)
HR (71)
RBI (883)
Hits (1625)
Runs (1129)
SLG (.456)
OBP (.351)
SB (354)

Rick Ferrell
St. Louis Browns, Boston Red Sox, Washington Senators (1929-1947)

AVG (.281) AB (6028)
HR (28)
RBI (734)
Hits (1692)
Runs (687)
SLG (.363)
OBP (.378)
SB (29)

Carlton Fisk
Boston Red Sox-Chicago White Sox
(1969-1993)

AVG (.269) AB (8756)
HR (376)
RBI (1330)
Hits (2356)
Runs (1276)
SLG (.457)
OBP (.370)
SB (128)

Gabby Hartnett
Chicago Cubs-New York Giants
(1922-1941)

AVG (.297) AB (6432)
HR (236)
RBI (990)
Hits (1912)
Runs (867)
SLG (.489)
OBP (.370)
SB (28)

Ernie Lombardi
Brooklyn Robins-Cincinnati Reds-Boston Braves-New York Giants
(1931-1947)

AVG (.306) AB (5855)
HR (190)
RBI (990)
Hits (1792)
Runs (601)
SLG (.460)
OBP (.358)
SB (8)

Ray Schalk
Chicago White Sox-New York Giants
(1912-1929)

AVG (.253) AB (5306)
HR (11)
RBI (594)
Hits (1345)
Runs (579)
SLG (.316)
OBP (.340)
SB (177)

FIRST BASEMEN

**Cap Anson
Jake Beckley
Jim Bottomley
Dan Brouthers
Orlando Cepeda
Frank Chance
Roger Connor
Jimmy Foxx
Lou Gehrig
Hank Greenberg
George Kelly
Harmon Killebrew
Willie McCover
Johnny Mize
Eddie Murray
Tony Perez
George Sisler
Bill Terry**
Thomas, Frank

Cap Anson
Chicago White Stockings-Chicago Colts
(1876-1897)

**AVG (.329) AB (10,281)
HR (97)
RBI (1879)
Hits (2995)
Runs (1719)
SLG (.446)
OBP (.395)
SB (247)**

Jake Beckley
Pittsburgh Alleghenys, Pittsburgh Burghers, Pittsburgh Pirates, New York Giants, Cincinnati Reds, St. Louis Cardinals
(1888-1907)

AVG (.308) AB (9538)
HR (86)
RBI (1575)
Hits (2930)
Runs (1600)
SLG (.435)
OBP (.361)
SB (315)

Jim Bottomley
St. Louis Cardinals, Cincinnati Reds, St. Louis Browns
(1922-1937)

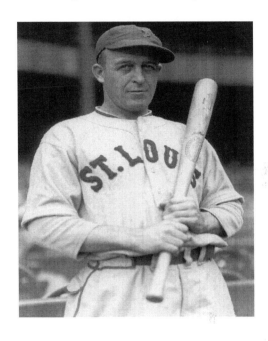

AVG (.310) AB (7471)
HR (219)
RBI (1422)
Hits (2313)
Runs (1177)
SLG (.500)
OBP (.369)
SB (58)

Dan Brouthers
Troy Trojans, Buffalo Bisons, Detroit Wolverines, Boston Beaneaters, Boston Red Stockings, Brooklyn Bridegrooms, Baltimore Orioles, Louisville Colonels, Philadelphia Phillies, New York Giants (1879-1904)

AVG (.342) AB (6711)
HR (106)
RBI (1296)
Hits (2296)
Runs (1523)
SLG (.519)
OBP (.423)
SB (256)

Orlando Cepeda
San Francisco Giants, St. Louis Cardinals, Atlanta Braves, Oakland Athletics, Boston Red Sox, Kansas City Royals
(1958-1974)

AVG (.297) AB (7927)
HR (379)
RBI (1365)
Hits (2351)
Runs (1131)
SLG (.499)
OBP (.353)
SB (142)

Frank Chance
Chicago Orphans, Chicago Cubs, New York Yankees
(1898-1914)

AVG (.296) AB (4299)
HR (20)
RBI (596)
Hits (1273)
Runs (797)
SLG (.394)
OBP (.394)
SB (401)

Roger Connor
Troy Trojans, New York Gothams, New York Giants, Philadelphia Phillies, St. Louis Browns
(1880-1897)

AVG (.317) AB (7797)
HR (138)
RBI (1322)
Hits (2467)
Runs (1620)
SLG (.486)
OBP (.397)
SB (244)

Jimmy Foxx
Philadelphia Athletics, Boston Red Sox, Chicago Cubs, Philadelphia Phillies (1925-1945)

AVG (.325) AB (8134)
HR (534)
RBI (1922)
Hits (2646)
Runs (1751)
SLG (.609)
OBP (.428)
SB (87)

Lou Gehrig
New York Yankees
(1923-1939)

AVG (.340) AB (8001)
HR (493)
RBI (1995)
Hits (2721)
Runs (1888)
SLG (.632)
OBP (.447)
SB (102)

Hank Greenberg
Detroit Tigers, Pittsburgh Pirates (1930-1947)

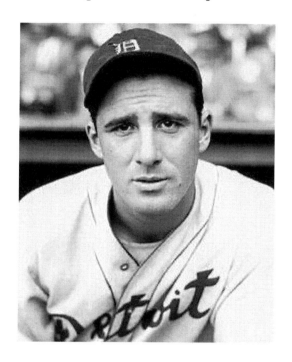

AVG (.313) AB (5193)
HR (331)
RBI (1276)
Hits (1628)
Runs (1051)
SLG (.605)
OBP (.412)
SB (58)

George Kelly
New York Giants, Pittsburgh Pirates, Cincinnati Reds, Chicago Cubs, Brooklyn Dodgers
(1915-1932)

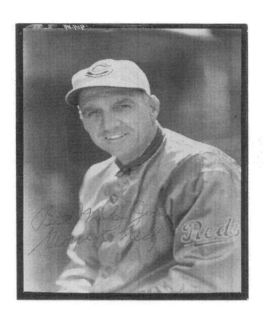

AVG (.297) AB (5993)
HR (148)
RBI (1020)
Hits (1778)
Runs (819)
SLG (.452)
OBP (.342)
SB (65)

Harmon Killebrew
Washington Senators, Minnesota Twins, Kansas City Royals
(1954-1975)

AVG (.256) AB (8147)
HR (573)
RBI (1584)
Hits (2086)
Runs (1283)
SLG (.509)
OBP (.379)
SB (19)

Willie McCovey
San Francisco Giants, San Diego Padres, Oakland Athletics
(1959-1980)

AVG (.270) AB (8197)
HR (521)
RBI (1555)
Hits (2211)
Runs (1229)
SLG (.515)
OBP (.377)
SB (26)

Johnny Mize
St. Louis Cardinals, New York Giants, New York Yankees
(1936-1953)

AVG (.312) AB (6443)
HR (359)
RBI (1337)
Hits (2011)
Runs (1118)
SLG (.562)
OBP (.397)
SB (28)

Eddie Murray
Baltimore Orioles, Los Angeles Dodgers, New York Mets, Cleveland Indians, Anaheim Angels
(1977-1997)

AVG (.287) AB (11,336)
HR (504)
RBI (1917)
Hits (3255)
Runs (1627)
SLG (.476)
OBP (.359)
SB (110)

Tony Perez
Cincinnati Reds, Montreal Expos, Boston Red Sox, Philadelphia Phillies
(1964-1986)

AVG (.279) AB (9778)
HR (379)
RBI (1652)
Hits (2732)
Runs (1272)
SLG (.463)
OBP (.344)
SB (49)

George Sisler
St. Louis Browns, Washington Senators, Boston Braves
(1915-1930)

AVG (.340) AB (8267)
HR (102)
RBI (1195)
Hits (2812)
Runs (1284)
SLG (.468)
OBP (.379)
SB (375)

Bill Terry
New York Giants
(1923-1936)

AVG (.341) AB (6428)
HR (154)
RBI (1078)
Hits (2193)
Runs (1120)
SLG (.506)
OBP (.393)
SB (56)

SECOND BASEMEN

Roberto Alomar
Rod Carew
Eddie Collins
Bobby Doerr
Johnny Evers
Nellie Fox
Frankie Frisch
Charlie Gehringer
Joe Gordon
Billy Herman
Rogers Hornsby
Napoleon Lajoie
Tony Lazzeri
Bill Mazeroski
Bid McPhee
Joe Morgan
Jackie Robinson
Ryne Sandberg
Red Schoenienst

Roberto Alomar
San Diego Padres, Toronto Blue Jays, Baltimore Orioles, Cleveland Indians, New York Mets, Chicago White Sox, Arizona Diamondbacks (1988-2004)

AVG (.300) (AB 9073)
HR (210)
RBI (1134)
Hits (2724)
Runs (1508)
SLG (.443)
OBP (.371)
SB (474)

Rod Carew
Minnesota Twins, California Angels
(1967-1985)

**AVG (.328) AB (9315)
HR (92)
RBI (1015)
Hits (3053)
Runs (1424)
SLG (.429)
OBP (.395)
SB (353)**

Eddie Collins
Philadelphia Athletics, Chicago White Sox (1906-1928)

AVG (.333) AB (9949)
HR (47)
RBI (1300)
Hits (3315)
Runs (1821)
SLG (.428)
OBP (.424)
SB (744)

Bobby Doerr
Boston Red Sox
(1937-1951)

AVG (.288) (AB 7093)
HR (223)
RBI (1247)
Hits (2042)
Runs (1094)
SLG (.461)
OBP (.362)
SB (54)

Johnny Evers
Chicago Cubs, Boston Braves, Philadelphia Phillies, Chicago White Sox
(1902-1929)

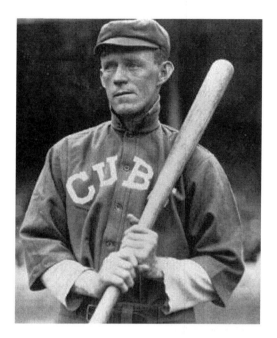

AVG (.270) AB (6137)
HR (12)
RBI (538)
Hits (1659)
Runs (919)
SLG (.334)
OBP (.356)
SB (324)

Nellie Fox
Philadelphia Athletics, Chicago White Sox, Houston Colt .45's, Houston Astros
(1947-1965)

AVG (.288) AB (9232)
HR (35)
RBI (790)
Hits (2663)
Runs (1279)
SLG (.432)
OBP (.349)
SB (76)

Frankie Frisch
New York Giants, St. Louis Cardinals
(1919-1937)

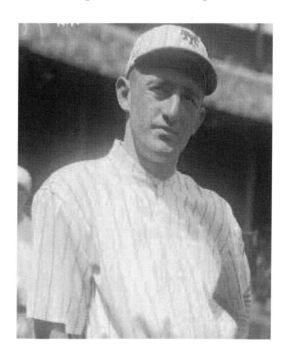

AVG (.316) AB (9112)
HR (105)
RBI (1244)
Hits (2880)
Runs (1532)
SLG (.432)
OBP (.369)
SB (419)

Charlie Gehringer
Detroit Tigers
(1924-1942)

**AVG (.320) AB (8860)
HR (184)
RBI (1427)
Hits (2839)
Runs (1774)
SLG (.480)
OBP (.404)
SB (181)**

Joe Gordon
New York Yankees, Cleveland Indians
(1938-1950)

AVG (.268) AB (5707)
HR (253)
RBI (975)
Hits (1530)
Runs (914)
SLG (.466)
OBP (.357)
SB (89)

Billy Herman
Chicago Cubs, Brooklyn Dodgers, Boston Braves, Pittsburgh Pirates
(1931-1947)

**AVG (.304) AB (7707)
HR (47)
RBI (839)
Hits (2345)
Runs (1163)
SLG (.407)
OBP (.367)
SB (67)**

Rogers Hornsby
St. Louis Cardinals, New York Giants, Boston Braves, Chicago Cubs, St. Louis Browns
(1915-1937)

AVG (.358) AB (8173)
HR (301)
RBI (1584)
Hits (2930)
Runs (1579)
SLG (.577)
OBP (.434)
SB (135)

Napoleon Lajoie
Philadelphia Phillies, Philadelphia Athletics, Cleveland Blues, Cleveland Naps
(1896-1916)

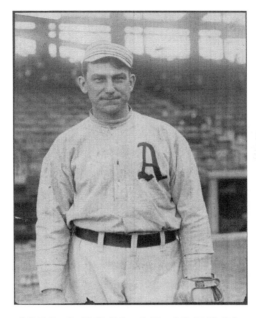

AVG (.339) AB (9589)
HR (83)
RBI (1599)
Hits (3242)
Runs (1504)
SLG (.467)
OBP (.380)
SB (380)

Tony Lazzeri
New York Yankees, Chicago Cubs, Brooklyn Dodgers, New York Giants
(1926-1939)

AVG (.292) AB (6297)
HR (178)
RBI (1191)
Hits (1840)
Runs (986)
SLG (.467)
OBP (.380)
SB (148)

Bill Mazeroski
Pittsburgh Pirates
(1956-1972)

AVG (.260) AB (7755)
HR (138)
RBI (853)
Hits (2016)
Runs (769)
SLG (.367)
OBP (.302)
SB (27)

Bid McPhee
Cincinnati Red Stockings, Cincinnati Reds (1882-1899)

**AVG (.271) AB (8291)
HR (53)
RBI (1067)
Hits (2250)
Runs (1678)
SLG (.372)
OBP (.355)
SB (568)**

David Furgess

Joe Morgan
Houston Colt .45's, Houston Astros, Cincinnati Reds, San Francisco Giants, Philadelphia Phillies, Oakland Athletics (1963-1984)

AVG (.271) AB (9277)
HR (268)
RBI (1133)
Hits (2517)
Runs (1650)
SLG (.427)
OBP (.395)
SB (689)

Jackie Robinson
Brooklyn Dodgers
(1947-1956)

AVG (.311) AB (4877)
HR (137)
RBI (734)
Hits (1518)
Runs (947)
SLG (.474)
OBP (.410)
SB (197)

Ryne Sandberg
Philadelphia Phillies, Chicago Cubs
(1981-1997)

AVG (.285) AB (8385)
HR (282)
RBI (1061)
Hits (2164)
Runs (1318)
SLG (.452)
OBP (.344)
SB (344)

Red Schoendienst
St. Louis Cardinals, New York Giants, Milwaukee Braves
(1945-1963)

AVG (.289) AB (8479)
HR (84)
RBI (773)
Hits (2449)
Runs (1223)
SLG (.387)
OBP (.338)
SB (89)

THIRD BASEMEN

**Frank Baker
Wade Boggs
George Brett
Jimmy Collins
George Kell
Freddie Lindstrom
Eddie Mathews
Brooks Robinson
Ron Santo
Mike Schmidt
Pie Traynor**

Frank "Home Run" Baker
Philadelphia Athletics, New York Yankees (1908-1922)

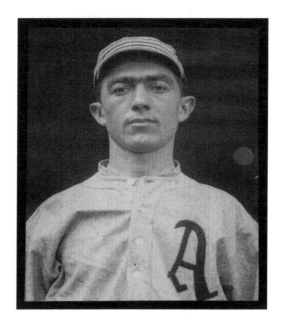

AVG (.307) AB (5984)
HR (96)
RBI (987)
Hits (1838)
Runs (887)
SLG (.442)
OBP (.363)
SB (235)

Wade Boggs
Boston Red Sox, New York Yankees, Tampa Bay Devil Rays
(1982-1999)

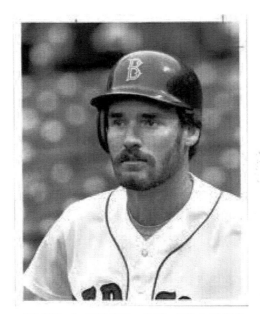

AVG (.328) AB (9180)
HR (118)
RBI (1014)
Hits (3010)
Runs (1513)
SLG (.443)
OBP (.415)
SB (24)

George Brett
Kansas City Royals
(1973-1993)

**AVG (.305) AB (10,349)
HR (317)
RBI (1595)
Hits (3154)
Runs (1583)
SLG (.487)
OBP (.373)
SB (201)**

Jimmy Collins
Boston Beaneaters, Louisville Colonels, Boston Americans, Philadelphia Athletics
(1895-1908)

AVG (.294) AB (6795)
HR (65)
RBI (983)
Hits (1999)
Runs (1055)
SLG (.409)
OBP (.344)
SB (194)

George Kell
Philadelphia Athletics, Detroit Tigers, Boston Red Sox, Chicago White Sox, Baltimore Orioles
(1943-1957)

AVG (.306) AB (6702)
HR (78)
RBI (870)
Hits (2054)
Runs (881)
SLG (.414)
OBP (.368)
SB (51)

Freddie Lindstrom
New York Giants, Pittsburgh Pirates, Chicago Cubs, Brooklyn Dodgers
(1924-1936)

AVG (.311) AB (5611)
HR (103)
RBI (779)
Hits (1747)
Runs (895)
SLG (.449)
OBP (.351)
SB (84)

Eddie Mathews
Boston Braves, Milwaukee Braves, Atlanta Braves, Houston Astros, Detroit Tigers (1952-1968)

AVG (.271) AB (8537)
HR (512)
RBI (1453)
Hits (2315)
Runs (1509)
SLG (.509)
OBP (.378)
SB (68)

Brooks Robinson
Baltimore Orioles
(1955-1977)

AVG (.267) AB (10,654)
HR (268)
RBI (1357)
Hits (2848)
Runs (1232)
SLG (.401)
OBP (.325)
SB (28)

Ron Santo
Chicago Cubs, Chicago White Sox
(1960-1974)

**AVG (.277) AB (8143)
HR (342)
RBI (1331)
Hits (2254)
Runs (1138)
SLG (.464)
OBP (.362)
SB (35)**

David Furgess

Mike Schmidt
Philadelphia Phillies
(1972-1989)

AVG (.267) AB (8352)
HR (548)*
RBI (1595)
Hits (2234)
Runs (1506)
SLG (.527)
OBP (.384)
SB (174)

Baseball Hall Of Famers By Position

Pie Traynor
Pittsburgh Pirates
(1920-1937)

AVG (.320) AB (7559)
HR (58)
RBI (1273)
Hits (2416)
Runs (1273)
SLG (.435)
OBP (.362)
SB (158)

SHORTSTOP

Luis Aparicio
Luke Appling
Dave Bancroft
Ernie Banks
Lou Boudreau
Joe Cronin
George Davis
Travis Jackson
Hughie Jennings
Barry Larkin
Rabbit Maranville
Pee Wee Reese
Cal Ripken Jr.
Phil Rizzuto
Joe Sewell
Ozzie Smith
Joe Tinker
Arky Vaughn
Honus Wagner
Bobby Wallace
John Ward
Robin Yount

Baseball Hall Of Famers By Position

Luis Aparicio
Chicago White Sox, Baltimore Orioles, Boston Red Sox

AVG (.262) AB (10,230)
HR (83)
RBI (791)
Hits (2677)
Runs (1335)
SLG (.343)
OBP (.311)
SB (506)

Luke Appling
Chicago White Sox
(1930-1950)

AVG (.310) AB (8856)
HR (45)
RBI (1116)
Hits (2749)
Runs (1319)
SLG (.398)
OBP (.310)
SB (179)

Dave Bancroft
Philadelphia Phillies, New York Giants, Boston Braves, Brooklyn Robins

AVG (.279) AB (7182)
HR (32)
RBI (591)
Hits (2004)
Runs (1048)
SLG (.358)
OBP (.355)
SB (145)

Ernie Banks
Chicago Cubs
(1953-1971)

**AVG (.274) AB (9421)
HR (512)
RBI (1636)
Hits (2583)
Runs (1305)
SLG (.500)
OBP (.330)
SB (50)**

Lou Boudreau
Cleveland Indians, Boston Red Sox
(1938-1952)

AVG (.295) AB (6029)
HR (68)
RBI (789)
Hits (1779)
Runs (861)
SLG (.415)
OBP (.380)
SB (51)

Joe Cronin
Pittsburgh Pirates, Washington Senators, Boston Red Sox
(1926-1945)

AVG (.301) AB (7579)
HR (170)
RBI (1424)
Hits (2285)
Runs (1233)
SLG (.468)
OBP (.390)
SB (87)

George Davis
Cleveland Spiders, New York Giants, Chicago White Sox
(1890-1909)

AVG (.295) AB (9045)
HR (73)
RBI (1440)
Hits (2665)
Runs (1545)
SLG (.405)
OBP (.362)
SB (619)

Travis Jackson
New York Giants
(1922-1936)

AVG (.291) AB (6086)
HR (135)
RBI (929)
Hits (1768)
Runs (833)
SLG (.433)
OBP (.337)
SB (71)

Hughie Jennings
Louisville Colonels, Baltimore Orioles, Brooklyn Superbas, Philadelphia Phillies, Detroit Tigers
(1891-1918)

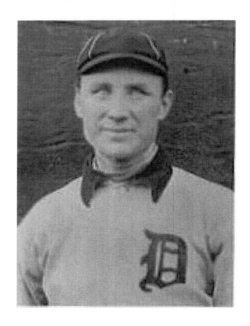

**AVG (.312) AB (4895)
HR (18)
RBI (840)
Hits (1526)
Runs (992)
SLG (.406)
OBP (.391)
SB (359)**

Barry Larkin
Cincinnati Reds
(1986-2004)

AVG (.295) AB (7937)
HR (198)
RBI (960)
Hits (2340)
Runs (1329)
SLG (.444)
OBP (.371)
SB (379)

Rabbit Maranville
Boston Braves, Pittsburgh Pirates, Chicago Cubs, Brooklyn Robins, St. Louis Cardinals
(1912-1935)

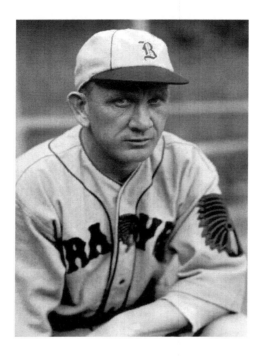

BA (.258) AB (10,078)
HR (28)
RBI (884)
Hits (2605)
Runs (1255)
SLG (.340)
OBP (.318)
SB (291)

David Furgess

Pee Wee Reese
Brooklyn Dodgers, Los Angeles Dodgers
1940-1958

AVG (.269) AB (8058)
HR (126)
RBI (885)
Hits (2170)
Runs (1338)
SLG (.377)
OBP (.366)
SB (232)

Baseball Hall Of Famers By Position

Cal Ripken Jr.
Baltimore Orioles
(1981-2001)

AVG (.276) AB (11,551)
HR (431)
RBI (1695)
Hits (3184)
Runs (1647)
SLG (.447)
OBP (.340)
SB (36)

Phil Rizzuto
New York Yankees
(1941-1956)

AVG (.273) AB (5816)
HR (38)
RBI (563)
Hits (1588)
Runs (877)
SLG (.355)
OBP (.351)
SB (149)

Joe Sewell
Cleveland Indians, New York Yankees
(1920-1933)

AVG (.312) AB (7132)
HR (49)
RBI (1054)
Hits (2226)
Runs (1141)
SLG (.413)
OBP (.391)
SB (74)

David Furgess

Ozzie Smith
San Diego Padres, St. Louis Cardinals
(1978-1996)

AVG (.262) AB (9396)
HR (28)
RBI (793)
Hits (2460)
Runs (1257)
SLG (.328)
OBP (.337)
SB (580)

Joe Tinker
Chicago Cubs, Chicago Orphans, Chicago Whales, Chicago Chi-Feds, Cincinnati Reds
(1902-1916)

AVG (.262) AB (6441)
HR (31)
RBI (783)
Hits (1690)
Runs (774)
SLG (.353)
OBP (.308)
SB (336)

Arky Vaughan
Pittsburgh Pirates, Brooklyn Dodgers
(1932-1948)

AVG (.318) AB (6622)
HR (96)
RBI (926)
Hits (2103)
Runs (1173)
SLG (.453)
OBP (.406)
SB (118)

Honus Wagner
Pittsburgh Pirates, Louisville Colonels
(1897-1917)

AVG (.328) (AB 10,439)
HR (101)
RBI (1733)
Hits (3420)
Runs (1739)
SLG (.467)
OBP (.391)
SB (723)

Bobby Wallace
Cleveland Spiders, St. Louis Perfectos, St. Louis Browns, St. Louis Cardinals
(1894-1918)

AVG (.268) AB (8618)
HR (34)
RBI (1121)
Hits (2309)
Runs (1057)
SLG (.358)
OBP (.332)
SB (201)

John Montgomery Ward
Providence Grays, New York Gothams, New York Giants, Brooklyn Ward's Wonders, Brooklyn Grooms
(1878-1894)

AVG (.275) AB (7656)
HR (26)
RBI (869)
Hits (2107)
Runs (1410)
SLG (.341)
OBP (.314)
SB (540)

Robin Yount
Milwaukee Brewers
(1974-1993)

AVG (.285) AB (11,008)
HR (251)
RBI (1406)
Hits (3142)
Runs (1632)
SLG (.430)
OBP (.342)
SB (271)

LEFT FIELDERS

**Lou Brock
Jesse Burkett
Fred Clarke
Ed Delahanty
Goose Goslin
Chick Hafey
Rickey Henderson
Joe Kelley
Ralph Kiner
Heinie Manush
Joe Medwick
Stan Musial
Jim Rice
Jim O'Rourke
Al Simmons
Willie Stargell
Zach Wheat
Billy Williams
Ted Williams
Carl Yastrzemski**

Lou Brock
Chicago Cubs, St. Louis Cardinals
(1961-1979)

AVG (.293) AB (10,332)
HR (149)
RBI (900)
Hits (3023)
Runs (1610)
SLG (.410)
OBP (.343)
SB (938)

Jesse Burkett
New York Giants, Cleveland Spiders, St. Louis Perfectos, St. Louis Cardinals, St. Louis Browns, Boston Americans (1890-1905)

AVG (.338) AB (8421)
HR (75)
RBI (952)
Hits (2850)
Runs (1720)
SLG (.446)
OBP (.415)
SB (389)

Fred Clarke
Louisville Colonels, Pittsburgh Pirates
(1894-1915)

AVG (.312) AB (8568)
HR (67)
RBI (1015)
Hits (2672)
Runs (1619)
SLG (.429)
OBP (.386)
SB (506)

Ed Delahanty
Philadelphia Phillies, Cleveland Infants, Washington Senators
(1888-1903)

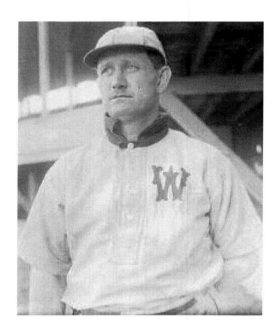

AVG (.346) AB (7505)
HR (101)
RBI (1464)
Hits (2596)
Runs (1599)
SLG (.505)
OBP (.411)
SB (455)

Goose Goslin
Washington Senators, St. Louis Browns, Detroit Tigers
(1921-1938)

AVG (.316) AB (8656)
HR (248)
RBI (1609)
Hits (2735)
Runs (1483)
SLG (.500)
OBP (.387)
SB (175)

Chick Hafey
St. Louis Cardinals, Cincinnati Reds
(1924-1937)

AVG (.317) AB (4625)
HR (164)
RBI (833)
Hits (1466)
Runs (777)
SLG (.526)
OBP (.372)
SB (70)

Rickey Henderson
Oakland Athletics, New York Yankees, Toronto Blue Jays, San Diego Padres, Anaheim Angels, New York Mets, Seattle Mariners, Boston Red Sox, Los Angeles Dodgers
(1979-2003)

AVG (.279) AB (10,961)
HR (297)
RBI (1115)
Hits (3055)
Runs (2295)
SLG (.419)
OBP (.401)
SB (1406)

Joe Kelley
Boston Beaneaters, Pittsburgh Pirates, Baltimore Orioles, Brooklyn Superbas, Cincinnati Reds, Boston Doves (1891-1908)

AVG (.317) AB (7006)
HR (65)
RBI (1194)
Hits (2220)
Runs (1421)
SLG (.451)
OBP (.402)
SB (443)

Ralph Kiner
Pittsburgh Pirates, Chicago Cubs, Cleveland Indians
(1946-1955)

AVG (.279) AB (5205)
HR (369)
RBI (1015)
Hits (1451)
Runs (971)
SLG (.548)
OBP (.398)
SB (22)

Heinie Manush
Detroit Tigers, St. Louis Browns, Washington Senators, Boston Red Sox, Brooklyn Dodgers, Pittsburgh Pirates (1923-1939)

AVG (.330) AB (7654)
HR (110)
RBI (1183)
Hits (2524)
Runs (1287)
SLG (.479)
OBP (.377)
SB (114)

Joe "Ducky" Medwick
St. Louis Cardinals, Brooklyn Dodgers, New York Giants, Boston Braves (1932-1948)

AVG (.324) AB (7635)
HR (205)
RBI (1383)
Hits (2471)
Runs (1198)
SLG (.505)
OBP (.362)
SB (42)

Stan Musial
St. Louis Cardinals
(1941-1963)

AVG (.331) AB (10,972)
HR (475)
RBI (1951)
Hits (3630)
Runs (1949)
SLG (.559)
OBP (.417)
SB (78)

Jim Rice
Boston Red Sox
(1974-1989)

AVG (.298) AB (8225)
HR (382)
RBI (1451)
Hits (2452)
Runs (1249)
SLG (.502)
OBP (.352)
SB (58)

Jim O'Rourke
Boston Red Caps, Providence Grays, Buffalo Bisons, New York Giants, Washington Senators
(1876-1904)

AVG (.307) AB (7399)
HR (50)
RBI (1010)
Hits (2268)
Runs (1446)
SLG (.418)
OBP (.352)
SB (191)

Al Simmons
Philadelphia Athletics, Chicago White Sox, Detroit Tigers, Washington Senators, Boston Bees, Cincinnati Reds, Boston Red Sox
(1924-1944)

AVG (.334) AB (8759)
HR (307)
RBI (1827)
Hits (2927)
Runs (1507)
SLG (.535)
OBP (.380)
SB (88)

Willie Stargell
Pittsburgh Pirates
(1962-1982)

AVG (.282) AB (7927)
HR (475)
RBI (1540)
Hits (2232)
Runs (1195)
SLG (.529)
OBP (.360)
SB (17)

Zach Wheat
Brooklyn Superbas, Brooklyn Dodgers, Brooklyn Robins, Philadelphia Athletics (1909-1927)

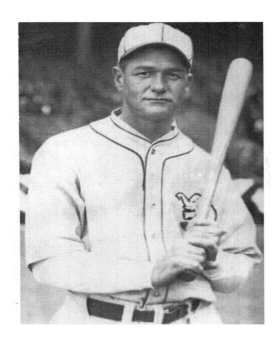

AVG (.317) AB (9106)
HR (132)
RBI (1248)
Hits (2884)
Runs (1289)
SLG (.450)
OBP (.367)
SB (205)

Billy Williams
Chicago Cubs, Oakland Athletics
(1959-1976)

**AVG (.290) AB (9350)
HR (426)
RBI (1475)
Hits (2711)
Runs (1410)
SLG (.492)
OBP (.361)
SB (90)**

Ted Williams
Boston Red Sox
(1939-1960)

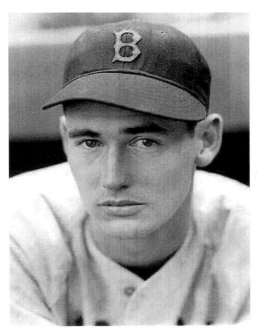

AVG (.344) AB (7706)
HR (521)
RBI (1839)
Hits (2654)
Runs (1798)
SLG (.634)
OBP (.482)
SB (24)

Carl Yastrzemski
Boston Red Sox
(1961-1983)

AVG (.285) AB (11,988)
HR (452)
RBI (1844)
Hits (3419)
Runs (1816)
SLG (.462)
OBP (.379)
SB (168)

Center Fielders

Richie Ashburn
Earl Averill
Max Carey
Ty Cobb
Earle Combs
Joe DiMaggio
Larry Doby
Hugh Duffy
Billy Hamilton
Mickey Mantle
Willie Mays
Kirby Puckett
Edd Roush
Duke Snider
Tris Speaker
Lloyd Waner
Hack Wilson

Richie Ashburn
Philadelphia Phillies, Chicago Cubs, New York Mets
(1948-1962)

AVG (.308) AB (8365)
HR (29)
RBI (586)
Hits (2574)
Runs (1322)
SLG (.382)
OBP (.396)
SB (234)

Earl Averill
Cleveland Indians, Detroit Tigers, Boston Braves
(1929-1941)

AVG (.318) AB (6353)
HR (238)
RBI (1164)
Hits (2019)
Runs (1224)
SLG (.534)
OBP (.395)
SB (70)

Max Carey
Pittsburgh Pirates, Brooklyn Robins
(1910-1929)

AVG (.285) AB (9363)
HR (70)
RBI (800)
Hits (2665)
Runs (1545)
SLG (.386)
OBP (.361)
SB (738)

Ty Cobb
Detroit Tigers, Philadelphia Athletics
(1905-1928)

AVG (.366) AB (11,434)
HR (117)
RBI (1937)
Hits (4189)
Runs (2246)
SLG (.512)
OBP (.433)
SB (892)

Earle Combs
New York Yankees
(1924-1935)

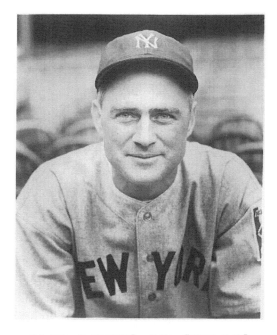

AVG (.325) AB (5746)
HR (58)
RBI (632)
Hits (1866)
Runs (1186)
SLG (.462)
OBP (.397)
SB (96)

Joe DiMaggio
New York Yankees
(1936-1951)

**AVG (.325) AB (6831)
HR (361)
RBI (1537)
Hits (2214)
Runs (1390)
SLG (.579)
OBP (.398)
SB (30)**

Larry Doby
Cleveland Indians, Chicago White Sox, Detroit Tigers
(1947-1959)

AVG (.283) AB (5348)
HR (253)
RBI (970)
Hits (1515)
Runs (960)
SLG (.490)
OBP (.386)
SB (47)

Hugh Duffy
Chicago White Stockings, Pittsburgh Pirates, Boston Beaneaters, Milwaukee Brewers, Philadelphia Phillies
(1888-1906)

AVG (.324) AB (7042)
HR (106)
RBI (1302)
Hits (2282)
Runs (1552)
SLG (.449)
OBP (.384)
SB (574)

Billy Hamilton
Cleveland Blues, Philadelphia Phillies, Boston Beaneaters
(1888-1901)

**AVG (.344) AB (6268)
HR (40)
RBI (736)
Hits (2158)
Runs (1690)
SLG (.432)
OBP (.455)
SB (912)**

David Furgess

Mickey Mantle
New York Yankees
(1951-1968)

AVG (.298) AB (8102)
HR (536)
RBI (1509)
Hits (2415)
Runs (1676)
SLG (.557)
OBP (.421)
SB (153)

Baseball Hall Of Famers By Position

Willie Mays
New York Giants, San Francisco Giants, New York Mets
(1951-1973)

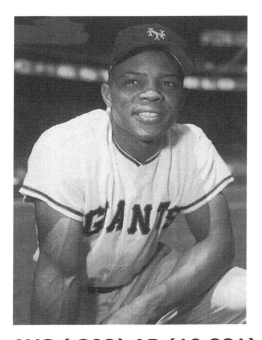

AVG (.302) AB (10,881)
HR (660)
RBI (1903)
Hits (3283)
Runs (2062)
SLG (.557)
OBP (.384)
SB (338)

David Furgess

Kirby Puckett
Minnesota Twins
(1984-1995)

AVG (.318) AB (7244)
HR (207)
RBI (1085)
Hits (2304)
Runs (1071)
SLG (.477)
OBP (.360)
SB (134)

Edd Roush
Chicago White Sox, Indianapolis Hoosiers, Newark Peppers, New York Giants, Cincinnati Reds
(1913-1931)

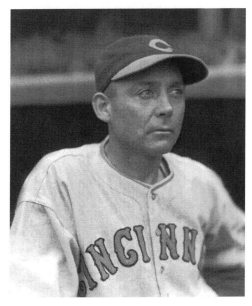

AVG (.323) AB (7363)
HR (68)
RBI (981)
Hits (2376)
Runs (1099)
SLG (.446)
OBP (.369)
SB (268)

Duke Snider
Brooklyn Dodgers, Los Angeles Dodgers, New York Mets, San Francisco Giants
(1947-1964)

AVG (.295) AB (7161)
HR (407)
RBI (1333)
Hits (2116)
Runs (1259)
SLG (.540)
OBP (.380)
SB (99)

Tris Speaker
Boston Americans, Boston Red Sox, Cleveland Indians, Washington Senators, Philadelphia Athletics
(1907-1928)

AVG (.345) AB (10,195)
HR (117)
RBI (1529)
Hits (3514)
Runs (1882)
SLG (.500)
OBP (.428)
SB (432)

Lloyd Waner
Pittsburgh Pirates, Boston Braves, Cincinnati Reds, Philadelphia Phillies, Brooklyn Dodgers
(1927-1945)

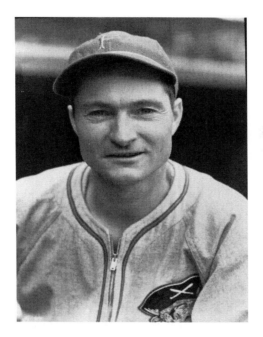

AVG (.316) AB (7772)
HR (27)
RBI (598)
Hits (2459)
Runs (1201)
SLG (.393)
OBP (.353)
SB (67)

Hack Wilson
New York Giants, Chicago Cubs, Brooklyn Dodgers, Philadelphia Phillies (1923-1934)

AVG (.307) AB (4760)
HR (244)
RBI (1063)
Hits (1461)
Runs (884)
SLG (.545)
OBP (.395)
SB (52)

Right Fielders

Hank Aaron
Roberto Clemente
Sam Crawford
Kiki Cuyler
Andre Dawson
Elmer Flick
Tony Gywnn
Harry Heilmann
Harry Hooper
Reggie Jackson
Al Kaline
Willie Keeler
King Kelly
Chuck Klein
Tommy McCarthy
Mel Ott
Sam Rice
Frank Robinson
Babe Ruth
Enos Slaughter
Sam Thompson
Paul Waner
Dave Winfield
Ross Youngs

Henry Aaron
Milwaukee Braves, Atlanta Braves, Milwaukee Brewers
(1954-1976)

AVG (.305) AB (12,364)
HR (755)
RBI (2297)
Hits (3771)
Runs (2174)
SLG (.555)
OBP (.374)
SB (240)

Roberto Clemente
Pittsburgh Pirates
(1955-1972)

AVG (.317) AB (9454)
HR (240)
RBI (1305)
Hits (3000)
Runs (1416)
SLG (.475)
OBP (.359)
SB (83)

Baseball Hall Of Famers By Position

Sam Crawford
Cincinnati Reds, Detroit Tigers
(1899-1917)

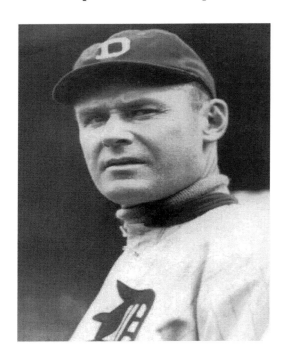

AVG (.309) AB (9570)
HR (97)
RBI (1525)
Hits (2961)
Runs (1391)
SLG (.452)
OBP (.362)
SB (366)

Kiki Cuyler
Pittsburgh Pirates, Chicago Cubs, Cincinnati Reds
(1921-1938)

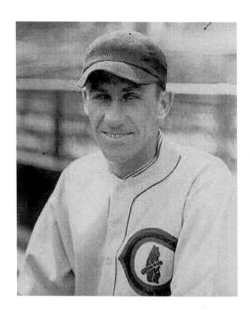

AVG (.321) AB (7161)
HR (128)
RBI (1065)
Hits (2299)
Runs (1305)
SLG (.474)
OBP (.386)
SB (328)

Andre Dawson
Montreal Expos, Chicago Cubs, Boston Red Sox, Florida Marlins
(1976-1996)

AVG (.279) AB (9927)
HR (438)
RBI (1591)
Hits (2774)
Runs (1373)
SLG (.482)
OBP (.323)
SB (314)

Elmer Flick
Philadelphia Phillies, Philadelphia Athletics, Cleveland Blues, Cleveland Naps
(1898-1910)

AVG (.313)
HR (48)
RBI (756)
Hits (1752)
Runs (950)
SLG (.445)
OBP (.389)
SB (330)

Tony Gwynn
San Diego Padres
(1982-2001)

AVG (.338) AB (9288)
HR (135)
RBI (1138)
Hits (3141)
Runs (1383)
SLG (.459)
OBP (.388)
SB (319)

Harry Heilmann
Detroit Tigers, Cincinnati Reds
(1914-1932)

AVG (.342) AB (7787)
HR (183)
RBI (1539)
Hits (2660)
Runs (1291)
SLG (.520)
OBP (.410)
SB (113)

Harry Hooper
Boston Red Sox, Chicago White Sox
(1909-1925)

AVG (.281) AB (8785)
HR (75)
RBI (817)
Hits (2466)
Runs (1429)
SLG (.387)
OBP (.368)
SB (375)

Reggie Jackson
Kansas City Athletics, Oakland Athletics, Baltimore Orioles, New York Yankees, California Angels
(1967-1987)

AVG (.262) AB (9864)
HR (563)
RBI (1702)
Hits (2584)
Runs (1551)
SLG (.490)
OBP (.356)
SB (228)

Al Kaline
Detroit Tigers
(1953-1974)

**AVG (.297) AB (10,116)
HR (399)
RBI (1583)
Hits (3007)
Runs (1622)
SLG (.480)
OBP (.376)
SB (137)**

Willie Keeler
New York Giants, Brooklyn Bridegrooms, Baltimore Orioles, Brooklyn Superbas, New York Highlanders
(1892-1910)

AVG (.341) AB (8591)
HR (33)
RBI (810)
Hits (2932)
Runs (1719)
SLG (.415)
OBP (.388)
SB (495)

King Kelly
Cincinnati Reds, Chicago White Stockings, Boston Beaneaters, Boston Red Stockings, Cincinnati Porkers, New York Giants
(1878-1893)

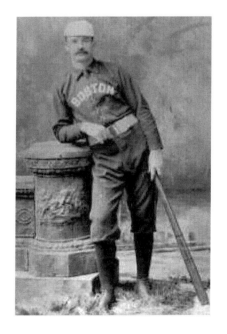

AVG (.301) AB (5839)
HR (69)
RBI (950)
Hits (1758)
Runs (1357)
SLG (.433)
OBP (.362)
SB (368)

Chuck Klein
Philadelphia Phillies, Chicago Cubs, Pittsburgh Pirates
(1928-1944)

AVG (.320) AB (6486)
HR (300)
RBI (1201)
Hits (2076)
Runs (1168)
SLG (.543)
OBP (.379)
SB (79)

Tommy McCarthy
Boston Unions, Boston Beaneaters, St. Louis Browns, Brooklyn Bridegrooms (1884-1896)

AVG (.291) AB (5126)
HR (44)
RBI (735)
Hits (1494)
Runs (1069)
SLG (.375)
OBP (.364)
SB (468)

Mel Ott
New York Giants
(1926-1947)

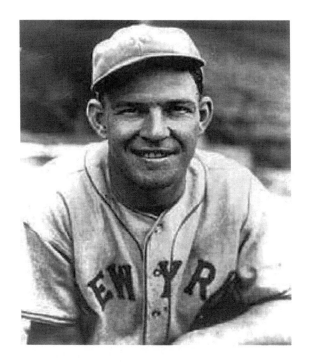

**AVG (.304) AB (9456)
HR (511)
RBI (1860)
Hits (2876)
Runs (1859)
SLG (.533)
OBP (.414)
SB (89)**

Sam Rice
Washington Senators, Cleveland Indians
(1915-1934)

**AVG (.322) AB (9269)
HR (34)
RBI (1078)
Hits (2987)
Runs (1514)
SLG (.427)
OBP (.374)
SB (351)**

Frank Robinson
Cincinnati Redlegs, Cincinnati Reds, Baltimore Orioles, Los Angeles Dodgers, California Angels, Cleveland Indians
(1956-1976)

AVG (.294) AB (10,006)
HR (586)
RBI (1812)
Hits (2943)
Runs (1829)
SLG (.537)
OBP (.389)
SB (204)

Babe Ruth
Boston Red Sox, New York Yankees, Boston Braves
(1914-1935)

AVG (.342) AB (8399)
HR (714)
RBI (2213)
Hits (2873)
Runs (2174)
SLG (.690)
OBP (.464)
SB (123)

Enos Slaughter
St. Louis Cardinals, New York Yankees, Kansas City Athletics, Milwaukee Braves
(1938-1959)

AVG (.300) AB (7946)
HR (169)
RBI (1304)
Hits (2383)
Runs (1247)
SLG (.453)
OBP (.382)
SB (71)

Sam Thompson
Detroit Wolverines, Philadelphia Phillies, Detroit Tigers
(1885-1906)

**AVG (.327) AB (5952)
HR (127)
RBI (1299)
Hits (1947)
Runs (1256)
SLG (.502)
OBP (.381)
SB (229)**

Paul Waner
Pittsburgh Pirates, Brooklyn Dodgers, Boston Braves, New York Yankees
(1926-1945)

AVG (.333) AB (9459)
HR (113)
RBI (1309)
Hits (3152)
Runs (1627)
SLG (.473)
OBP (.404)
SB (104)

Dave Winfield
San Diego Padres, New York Yankees, California Angels, Toronto Blue Jays, Minnesota Twins, Cleveland Indians (1973-1995)

AVG (.283) AB (11,003)
HR (465)
RBI (1833)
Hits (3110)
Runs (1669)
SLG (.475)
OBP (.353)
SB (223)

Ross Youngs
New York Giants
(1917-1926)

**AVG (.322) AB (4627)
HR (42)
RBI (592)
Hits (1491)
Runs (812)
SLG (.441)
OBP (.399)
SB (153)**

Baseball Hall Of Famers By Position

Pitchers

Pete "Grover Cleveland" Alexander
Chief Bender
Mordecai "Three Finger" Brown
Jim Bunning
Steve Carlton
Jack Chesbro
John Clarkson
Stan Coveleski
Candy Cummings
Dizzy Dean
Don Drysdale
Dennis Eckersley
Red Faber
Bob Feller
Rollie Fingers
Whitey Ford
Pud Galvin
Bob Gibson
Tom Glavine
Lefty Gomez
Rich "Goose" Gossage
Burleigh Grimes
Lefty Grove
Jesse Haines
Waite Hoyt
Carl Hubbell
Jim "Catfish" Hunter
Ferguson Jenkins
Walter Johnson

Pitchers (cont.)

Addie Joss
Tim Keefe
Sandy Koufax
Bob Lemon
Ted Lyons
Greg Maddux
Juan Marichal
Rube Marquard
Christy Mathewson
Joe McGinnity
Hal Newhouser
Kid Nichols
Phil Niekro
Jim Palmer
Herb Pennock
Gaylord Perry
Eddie Plank
Old Hoss Radbourn
Eppa Rixey
Robin Roberts
Red Ruffing
Amos Rusie
Nolan Ryan
Tom Seaver
Hilton Smith
Warren Spahn
Bruce Sutter
Don Sutton
Dazzy Vance

Pitchers (cont.)

Rube Waddell
Ed Walsh
Mickey Welch
Hoyt Wilhelm
Vic Willis
Early Wynn
Cy Young

David Furgess

Grover Cleveland Alexander RHP
Philadelphia Phillies, Chicago Cubs, St. Louis Cardinals
(1911-1930)

Wins (373)
Losses (208)
Pct. (.642)
ERA (256)
CG (437)
Strikeouts (2198)
Saves (32)
IP (5090)
Hits (4868)

Chief Bender RHP
Philadelphia Athletics, Baltimore Terrapins, Philadelphia Phillies, Chicago White Sox
(1903-1925)

Wins (212)
Losses (127)
Pct. (.625)
ERA (2.46)
CG (255)
Strikeouts (1711)
Saves (34)
IP (3017)
Hits (2645)

David Furgess

Mordecai "Three Finger" Brown RHP
St. Louis Cardinals, Chicago Cubs, Cincinnati Reds, Brooklyn Tip Tops, St. Louis Terriers, Chicago Whales (1903-1916)

Wins (239)
Losses (130)
Pct. (.648)
ERA (2.06)
CG (271)
Strikeouts (1375)
Saves (49)
IP (3172.1)
Hits (2708)

Jim Bunning RHP
Detroit Tigers, Philadelphia Phillies, Pittsburgh Pirates, Los Angeles Dodgers (1955-1971)

Wins (224)
Losses (184)
Pct. (.549)
ERA (3.27)
CG (151)
Strikeouts (2855)
Saves (16)
IP (3760.1)
Hits (3433)

Steve Carlton LHP
St. Louis Cardinals, Philadelphia Phillies, San Francisco Giants, Chicago White Sox, Cleveland Indians, Minnesota Twins (1965-1988)

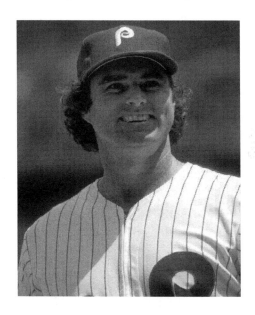

Wins (329)
Losses (244)
Pct. (.574)
ERA (3.22)
CG (254)
Strikeouts (4136)
Saves (2)
IP (5217.1)
Hits (4672)

Jack Chesbro RHP
Pittsburgh Pirates, New York Highlanders, Boston Red Sox (1899-1909)

Wins (198)
Losses (132)
Pct. (.600)
ERA (2.68)
CG (260)
Strikeouts (1265)
Saves (5)
IP (2896.1)
Hits (2642)

John Clarkson RHP
Worcester Ruby Legs, Chicago White Stockings, Boston Beaneaters, Cleveland Spiders
(1882-1894)

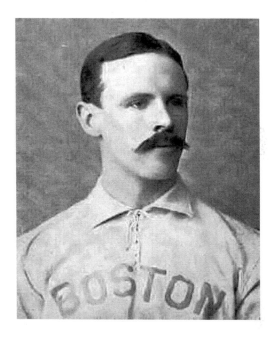

Wins (328)
Losses (178)
Pct. (.648)
ERA (2.81)
CG (485)
Strikeouts (1978)
Saves (5)
IP (4536.1)
Hits (4295)

Stan Coveleski RHP
Philadelphia Athletics, Cleveland Indians, Washington Senators, New York Yankees (1912-1928)

Wins (215)
Losses (142)
Pct. (.602)
ERA (2.89)
CG (224)
Strikeouts (981)
Saves (21)
IP (3082)
Hits (3055)

Candy Cummings
New York Mutuals, Baltimore Canaries, Philadelphia Whites, Hartford Dark Blues, Cincinnati Reds
(1872-1877)

Wins (145)
Losses (94)
Pct. (.607)
ERA (2.42)
CG (233)
Strikeouts (259)
Saves (0)
IP (2149.2)
Hits (2526)

Dizzy Dean RHP
St. Louis Cardinals, Chicago Cubs, St. Louis Browns
(1930-1947)

Wins (150)
Losses (83)
Pct. (.644)
ERA (3.02)
CG (154)
Strikeouts (1163)
Saves (30)
IP (1967.1)
Hits (1919)

Don Drysdale RHP
Brooklyn Dodgers, Los Angeles Dodgers
(1956-1969)

Wins (209)
Losses (166)
Pct. (.557)
ERA (2.95)
CG (167)
Strikeouts (2486)
Saves (6)
IP (3432.0)
Hits (3084)

Dennis Eckersley RHP
Cleveland Indians, Boston Red Sox, Chicago Cubs, Oakland Athletics, St. Louis Cardinals
(1975-1998)

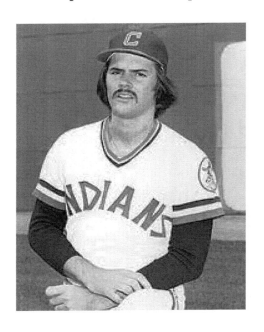

Wins (197)
Losses (171)
Pct. (.535)
ERA (3.50)
CG (100)
Strikeouts (2401)
Saves (390)
IP (3285.2)
Hits (3076)

Red Faber RHP
Chicago White Sox
(1914-1933)

Wins (254)
Losses (213)
Pct. (.544)
ERA (3.15)
CG (273)
Strikeouts (1471)
Saves (273)
IP (4086.2)
Hits (4106)

Bob Feller RHP
Cleveland Indians
(1936-1956)

Wins (266)
Losses (162)
Pct. (.621)
ERA (3.25)
CG (279)
Strikeouts (2581)
Saves (21)
IP (3827.0)
Hits (3271)

Rollie Fingers RHP
Oakland Athletics, San Diego Padres, Milwaukee Brewers
(1968-1985)

Wins (114)
Losses (118)
Pct. (.491)
ERA (2.90)
CG (4)
Strikeouts (1299)
Saves (341)
IP (1701.1)
Hits (1474)

Whitey Ford LHP
New York Yankees (1950-1967)

Wins (236)
Losses (106)
Pct. (.690)
ERA (2.75)
CG (156)
Strikeouts (1956)
Saves (10)
IP (3170.1)
Hits (2766)

James "Pud" Galvin RHP
St. Louis Brown Stockings, Buffalo Bisons, Pittsburgh Alleghenys, Pittsburgh Burghers, Pittsburgh Pirates, St. Louis Browns
(1875-1892)

Wins (365)
Losses (310)
Pct. (.541)
ERA (2.85)
CG (646)
Strikeouts (1807)
Saves (2)
IP (6003.1)
Hits (6405)

Bob Gibson RHP
St. Louis Cardinals
(1959-1975)

**Wins (251)
Losses (174)
Pct. (.591)
ERA (2.91)
CG (255)
Strikeouts (3117)
Saves (6)
IP (3884.1)
Hits (3279)**

Tom Glavine
Atlanta Braves, New York Mets
(1987-2008)

Wins (305)
Losses (203)
Pct. (.600)
ERA (3.54)
CG (56)
Strikeouts (2607)
Saves (0)
IP (4413.1)
Hits (4298)

Lefty Gomez LHP
New York Yankees, Washington Senators
(1930-1943)

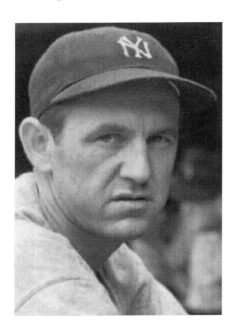

Wins (189)
Losses (102)
Pct. (.649)
ERA (3.34)
CG (173)
Strikeouts (1468)
Saves (9)
IP (2503)
Hits (2290)

Rich "Goose" Gossage RHP
Chicago White Sox, Pittsburgh Pirates, New York Yankees, San Diego Padres, Chicago Cubs, San Francisco Giants, Texas Rangers, Oakland Athletics, Seattle Mariners
(1972-1994)

Wins (124)
Losses (107)
Pct. (.537)
ERA (3.01)
CG (16)
Strikeouts (1502)
Saves (310)
IP (1809.1)
Hits (1497)

Burleigh Grimes RHP
Pittsburgh Pirates, Brooklyn Robins, New York Giants, Boston Braves, St. Louis Cardinals, Chicago Cubs, New York Yankees
(1916-1934)

Wins (270)
Losses (212)
Pct. (.560)
ERA (3.53)
CG (314)
Strikeouts (1512)
Saves (18)
IP (4180)
Hits (4412)

Lefty Grove LHP
Philadelphia Athletics, Boston Red Sox (1925-1941)

Wins (300)
Losses (141)
Pct. (.680)
ERA (3.06)
CG (298)
Strikeouts (2266)
Saves (55)
IP (3940.2)
Hits (3849)

Jesse Haines RHP
St. Louis Cardinals, Cincinnati Reds
(1918-1937)

Wins (210)
Losses (158)
Pct. (.571)
ERA (3.64)
CG (208)
Strikeouts (981)
Saves (10)
IP (3208.2)
Hits (3460)

Waite Hoyt RHP
New York Giants, Boston Red Sox, New York Yankees, Detroit Tigers, Philadelphia Athletics, Brooklyn Dodgers, Pittsburgh Pirates
(1918-1938)

Wins (237)
Losses (182)
Pct. (.566)
ERA (3.59)
CG (226)
Strikeouts (1206)
Saves (52)
IP (3762.1)
Hits (4037)

Carl Hubbell LHP
New York Giants
(1928-1943)

**Wins (253)
Losses (154)
Pct. (.622)
ERA (2.98)
CG (260)
Strikeouts (1677)
Saves (33)
IP (3590.1)
Hits (3461)**

Jim "Catfish" Hunter RHP
Kansas City Athletics, Oakland Athletics, New York Yankees
(1965-1979)

Wins (224)
Losses (166)
Pct. (.574)
ERA (3.26)
CG (181)
Strikeouts (2012)
Saves (1)
IP (3449.1)
Hits (2958)

Ferguson Jenkins RHP
Philadelphia Phillies, Chicago Cubs, Texas Rangers, Boston Red Sox
(1965-1983)

Wins (284)
Losses (226)
Pct. (.557)
ERA (3.34)
CG (267)
Strikeouts (3192)
Saves (7)
IP (4500.2)
Hits (4142)

Walter Johnson RHP
Washington Senators
(1907-1927)

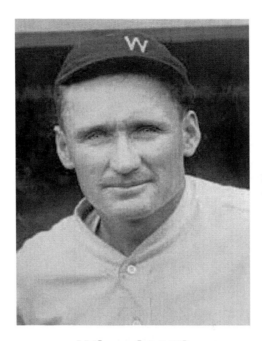

Wins (417)
Losses (279)
Pct. (.599)
ERA (2.17)
CG (531)
Strikeouts (3509)
Saves (34)
IP (5914.1)
Hits (4913)

Addie Joss RHP
Cleveland Bronchos, Cleveland Naps
(1902-1910)

Wins (160)
Losses (97)
Pct. (.623)
ERA (1.89)
CG (234)
Strikeouts (920)
Saves (5)
IP (2327)
Hits (1888)

Tim Keefe RHP
Troy Trojans, New York Metropolitans, New York Giants, Philadelphia Phillies (1990-1893)

Wins (342)
Losses (225)
Pct. (.603)
ERA (2.63)
CG (554)
Strikeouts (2564)
Saves (2)
IP (5049.2)
Hits (4438)

Sandy Koufax LHP
Brooklyn Dodgers, Los Angeles Dodgers
(1955-1966)

Wins (165)
Losses (87)
Pct. (.655)
ERA (2.76)
CG (137)
Strikeouts (2396)
Saves (9)
IP (2324.1)
Hits (1754)

Bob Lemon RHP
Cleveland Indians
(1941-1958)

Wins (207)
Losses (128)
Pct. (.618)
ERA (3.23)
CG (188)
Strikeouts (1277)
Saves (22)
IP (2850)
Hits (2559)

Ted Lyons RHP
Chicago White Sox
(1923-1946)

Wins (260)
Losses (230)
Pct. (.531)
ERA (3.67)
CG (356)
Strikeouts (1073)
Saves (23)
IP (4161)
Hits (4489)

Greg Maddux
Chicago Cubs, Atlanta Braves, Los Angeles Dodgers, San Diego Padres (1986-2008)

Wins (355)
Losses (227)
Pct. (.610)
ERA (3.16)
CG (109)
Strikeouts (3371)
Saves (0)
IP (5008.1)
Hits (4726)

Juan Marichal RHP
San Francisco Giants, Boston Red Sox, Los Angeles Dodgers
(1960-1975)

Wins (243)
Losses (142)
Pct. (.631)
ERA (2.89)
CG (244)
Strikeouts (2303)
Saves (2)
IP (3507)
Hits (3153)

Rube Marquard LHP
New York Giants, Brooklyn Robins, Cincinnati Reds, Boston Braves (1908-1925)

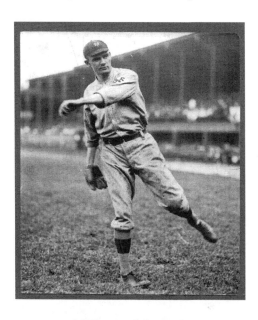

Wins (201)
Losses (177)
Pct. (.532)
ERA (3.08)
CG (197)
Strikeouts (1593)
Saves (19)
IP (3306.2)
Hits (3233)

Christy Mathewson RHP
Cincinnati Reds, New York Giants
(1900-1916)

**Wins (373)
Losses (188)
Pct. (.665)
ERA (2.13)
CG (435)
Strikeouts (2507)
Saves (30)
IP (4788.2)
Hits (4219)**

David Furgess

Joe McGinnity RHP
Baltimore Orioles, Brooklyn Superbas, New York Giants
(1899-1908)

Wins (246)
Losses (142)
Pct. (.634)
ERA (2.66)
CG (314)
Strikeouts (1068)
Saves (24)
IP (3441.1)
Hits (3276)

Baseball Hall Of Famers By Position

Hal Newhouser LHP
Detroit Tigers, Cleveland Indians (1939-1955)

**Wins (207)
Losses (150)
Pct. (.580)
ERA (3.06)
CG (212)
Strikeouts (1796)
Saves (26)
IP (2993)
Hits (2674)**

Kid Nichols RHP
Boston Beaneaters, St. Louis Cardinals, Philadelphia Phillies
(1890-1906)

Wins (361)
Losses (208)
Pct. (.634)
ERA (2.96)
CG (532)
Strikeouts (1881)
Saves (17)
IP (5067.1)
Hits (4929)

Phil Niekro RHP
Milwaukee Braves, Atlanta Braves, New York Yankees, Cleveland Indians, Toronto Blue Jays
(1964-1987)

Wins (318)
Losses (274)
Pct. (.537)
ERA (3.35)
CG (245)
Strikeouts (3342)
Saves (29)
IP (5404)
Hits (5044)

Jim Palmer RHP
Baltimore Orioles
(1965-1984)

Wins (268)
Losses (152)
Pct. (.638)
ERA (2.86)
CG (211)
Strikeouts (2212)
Saves (4)
IP (3948)
Hits (3349)

Herb Pennock LHP
Philadelphia Athletics, Boston Red Sox, New York Yankees
(1912-1934)

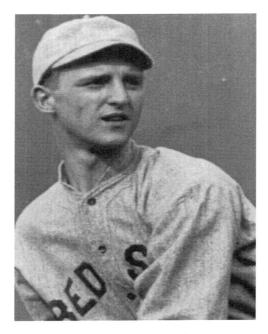

Wins (241)
Losses (162)
Pct. (.598)
ERA (3.60)
CG (247)
Strikeouts (1227)
Saves (33)
IP (3571.2)
Hits (3900)

Gaylord Perry RHP
San Francisco Giants, Cleveland Indians, Texas Rangers, San Diego Padres, New York Yankees, Atlanta Braves, Seattle Mariners, Kansas City Royals
(1962-1983)

Wins (314)
Losses (265)
Pct. (.542)
ERA (3.11)
CG (303)
Strikeouts (3534)
Saves (11)
IP (5350)
Hits (4938)

Eddie Plank LHP
Philadelphia Athletics, St. Louis Terriers, St. Louis Browns
(1901-1917)

Wins (326)
Losses (194)
Pct. (.627)
ERA (2.35)
CG (410)
Strikeouts (2246)
Saves (23)
IP (4495.2)
Hits (3958)

Charles "Old Hoss" Radbourn RHP
Providence Grays, Boston Beaneaters, Boston Reds, Cincinnati Reds
(1881-1891)

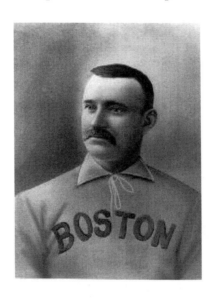

Wins (309)
Losses (194)
Pct. (.614)
ERA (2.68)
CG (488)
Strikeouts (1830)
Saves (3)
IP (4527.1)
Hits (4328)

Eppa Rixey LHP
Philadelphia Phillies, Cincinnati Reds
(1912-1933)

Wins (266)
Losses (251)
Pct. (.515)
ERA (3.15)
CG (290)
Strikeouts (1350)
Saves (14)
IP (4494.2)
Hits (4633)

Robin Roberts RHP
Philadelphia Phillies, Baltimore Orioles, Houston Astros, Chicago Cubs (1948-1966)

Wins (286)
Losses (245)
Pct. (.539)
ERA (3.41)
CG (305)
Strikeouts (2357)
Saves (25)
IP (4688.2)
Hits (4582)

Red Ruffing RHP
Boston Red Sox, New York Yankees, Chicago White Sox
(1924-1937)

Wins (273)
Losses (225)
Pct. (.548)
ERA (3.80)
CG (335)
Strikeouts (1987)
Saves (16)
IP (4344.0)
Hits (4284)

Amos Rusie RHP
New York Giants, Indianapolis Hoosiers, Cincinnati Reds
(1889-1901)

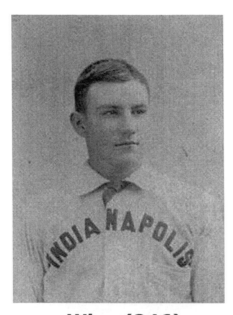

Wins (246)
Losses (174)
Pct. (.586)
ERA (3.07)
CG (393)
Strikeouts (1950)
Saves (5)
IP (3778.2)
Hits (3389)

Nolan Ryan RHP
New York Mets, California Angels, Houston Astros, Texas Rangers (1966-1993)

Wins (324)
Losses (292)
Pct. (.526)
ERA (3.19)
CG (222)
Strikeouts (5714)
Saves (3)
IP (5386.0)
Hits (3923)

David Furgess

Tom Seaver RHP
New York Mets, Cincinnati Reds, Chicago White Sox, Boston Red Sox
(1967-1986)

Wins (311)
Losses (205)
Pct. (.603)
ERA (2.86)
CG (231)
Strikeouts (3640)
Saves (1)
IP (4783.0)
Hits (3971)

Warren Spahn LHP
Boston Braves, Milwaukee Braves, New York Mets, San Francisco Giants (1942-1965)

Wins (363)
Losses (245)
Pct. (.597)
ERA (3.09)
CG (382)
Strikeouts (2583)
Saves (29)
IP (5243.2)
Hits (4830)

Bruce Sutter RHP
Chicago Cubs, St. Louis Cardinals, Atlanta Braves
(1976-1988)

Wins (68)
Losses (71)
Pct. (.489)
ERA (2.83)
CG (0)
Strikeouts (861)
Saves (300)
IP (1042)
Hits (879)

Don Sutton RHP
Los Angeles Dodgers, California Angels, Milwaukee Brewers, Houston Astros, Oakland Athletics
(1966-1988)

Wins (324)
Losses (256)
Pct. (.559)
ERA (3.26)
CG (178)
Strikeouts (3574)
Saves (5)
IP (5282.1)
Hits (4692)

Dazzy Vance RHP
Pittsburgh Pirates, New York Yankees, Brooklyn Robins, Brooklyn Dodgers, St. Louis Cardinals, Cincinnati Reds (1915-1935)

Wins (197)
Losses (140)
Pct. (.585)
ERA (3.24)
CG (216)
Strikeouts (2045)
Saves (11)
IP (2966.2)
Hits (2809)

Rube Waddell LHP
Louisville Colonels, Pittsburgh Pirates, Chicago Orphans, Philadelphia Athletics, St. Louis Browns
(1897-1910)

Wins (193)
Losses (143)
Pct. (.574)
ERA (2.16)
CG (261)
Strikeouts (2316)
Saves (5)
IP (2961.1)
Hits (2460)

David Furgess

Ed Walsh RHP
Chicago White Sox, Boston Braves
(1904-1917)

Wins (195)
Losses (126)
Pct. (.607)
ERA (1.82)
CG (250)
Strikeouts (1736)
Saves (35)
IP (2964.1)
Hits (2346)

Mickey Welch RHP
Troy Trojans, New York Gothams, New York Giants
(1880-1892)

**Wins (307)
Losses (210)
Pct. (.594)
ERA (2.71)
CG (525)
Strikeouts (1850)
Saves (4)
IP (4802)
Hits (4588)**

Hoyt Wilhelm RHP
New York Giants, St. Louis Cardinals, Cleveland Indians, Baltimore Orioles, Chicago White Sox, California Angels, Chicago Cubs, Los Angeles Dodgers (1952-1972)

Wins (143)
Losses (122)
Pct. (.540)
ERA (2.52)
CG (20)
Strikeouts (1610)
Saves (227)
IP (2254.1)
Hits (1757)

Baseball Hall Of Famers By Position

Vic Willis RHP
Boston Beaneaters, Pittsburgh Pirates, St. Louis Cardinals (1898-1910)

**Wins (249)
Losses (205)
Pct. (.548)
ERA (2.63)
CG (388)
Strikeouts (1651)
Saves (11)
IP (3996)
Hits (3621)**

David Furgess

Early Wynn RHP
Washington Senators, Cleveland Indians, Chicago White Sox
(1939-1963)

Wins (300)
Loses (244)
Pct. (.551)
ERA (3.54)
CG (290)
Strikeouts (2334)
Saves (15)
IP (4564)
Hits (4291)

Cy Young RHP
Cleveland Spiders, St. Louis Perfectos, Boston Americans, Boston Red Sox, Cleveland Naps, Boston Rustlers (1890-1911)

Wins (511)
Losses (316)
Pct. (.618)
ERA (2.63)
CG (749)
Strikeouts (2803)
Saves (17)
IP (7356)
Hits (7092)

About The Author

David Furgess was born in Bridgeport, Connecticut on February 27, 1961. He grew up a Chicago Cubs fan and still roots for them today. He is a season ticket holder for the Connecticut Tigers (Class A SS affiliate of the Detroit Tigers) who play at Dodd Stadium in Norwich, Connecticut. He currently runs a mail order business that deals in rare phonograph records at (autumn66records.blogspot.com)

David Furgess is also the author of:

Chicago Cubs Fact Book 2013

Chicago Cubs Minor League Report 2013

So You Call Yourself A Chicago Cubs Fan?

2013 Connecticut Tigers Annual

Municipal Stadium, Waterbury, Connecticut: The Way It Was

For more information on David Furgess' books please visit:

shibeparkpublishing.blogspot.com

Baseball Hall Of Famers By Position

Dedicated to Skippy The Cat!

David Furgess

Baseball Hall Of Famers By Position

Made in the USA
San Bernardino, CA
08 July 2014